THE END OF THE WORLD

First published in 2019 by
The Dedalus Press
13 Moyclare Road
Baldoyle
Dublin D13 K1C2
Ireland

www.**dedaluspress**.com

ISBN 978 1 910251 54 6 paperback
ISBN 978 1 910251 55 3 hardback

Dedalus Press titles are available in Ireland
from Argosy Books (argosybooks.ie) and in the UK
from Inpress Books (www.inpressbooks.co.uk)

Cover image: *Paraphernalia 1* (2019), Oil on canvas, 70 x 50 cm
by Judy Carroll Deeley, by kind permission of the artist

The Dedalus Press receives financial assistance from
The Arts Council / An Chomhairle Ealaíon.

THE END OF THE WORLD

PATRICK DEELEY

DEDALUS PRESS

Contents

∾

— 1—

The Ash Pit / 13
Two Hundred Million Animals / 15
Scribble Lark / 16
The Invisible Man / 17
Wild Barley / 18
Houses / 19
The Migration / 21
Poultice / 23
Fatherhood / 25
Half-carcass of Calf / 26
Render / 28
The Soldier on Clare Island / 30

— 2 —

A Fable / 35
Esther / 36
My Mother's Getaway / 37
Amcotts Moor Woman / 38
Towards a Frontier / 40
Boxes / 42
Renoir / 44
Contesting Cuckoos / 45
Cleft in Metal / 46
Budgerigar / 47
The tree growing inside a man's lung / 48
The Pull / 49
Shiners / 50
The Wedge / 51
Undercut / 52

— 3 —

The Refuse Gatherers / 57
Between / 59
Manhole Cover / 61
Disappearing Acts – A Street Triptych / 62
Starlings / 64
Anthony of the Desert / 65
North Mayo Haiku / 66
Torso / 67
Roaming Maamtrasna / 68
T. Rex Skull, Ulster Museum / 69
A Stopped Moment in Childhood / 70
The Victor / 71
Achilles Regrets / 72
Till the Next Time / 74

— 4 —

Precursor / 77
Toad / 79
Seals Conversing / 80
North Mayo Night / 81
The Boat / 83
Downpatrick Head / 84
Petrosmatoglyphs / 86
Travel / 87
Another Life / 88
In the Burncourt Cave / 90
Burials / 92
You Call It Charm / 95
However the Malady / 96
'Still it Moves' / 97
Vixen / 99

NOTES / 100
ACKNOWLEDGEMENTS / 101

for Judy, Alan and Genevieve, with love

The End of the World

They've nothing in common, the young girl knocked
from her bicycle and dying on a roadside
in Harold's Cross, and the tribesman of Sumatra
being interviewed on television, shaking
his head at the levelled forest, cut and burn stretching
for miles behind him; they've nothing in common

except, as the man says, the end of the world
is happening. And the sight of a green snake flicking
its tongue at a chainsaw that keeps cutting;
and the sight of a rainbow flourished above the city
after we look up from the crumpled shape
of the girl, both haunt us, being more than props

for pathos, more than backdrops to the uselessness
even of beauty in face of greed or misfortune.
The end of the world is happening, and grief that stands
sudden tears in our staring eyes might wish them
closed as soon, with no desire to open again –
but this, too, is the world, and somehow a beginning.

1

The Ash Pit

What if a hot coal caused the dead weeds,
the nettles and husks of Queen Anne's Lace,
to spark up and a flame to take hold

of the scabby pine tree that bowed
and scraped its existence from the ash pit?
This, the men said, humouring a child

full of questions, was what happened.
But what if the flame twisted into a red squirrel
climbing the trunk, twitching as he

fitted himself between branches?
Shush now, the men said, their hands busy
with implements and machines

splitting logs into planks in the long,
loud sawmill. But she who cleared the bucket
of ashes, the pisspots and eggshells,

the stale crusts from the bread bin
and the tired skins of eaten things, cleared them
every morning, said let nature sprout

a new nettle, turn a fresh dock leaf, open
the wings of a peacock butterfly, start a sapling
out of a cone dropped by the pine,

said nature could allow for its own design,
fireball or squirrel, fox, badger,
kangaroo, change even the 'salt-and-pepper'

Greenland geese that grazed
all winter in the Callows into flaming flamingos
if it had a mind to. Imagine, just imagine.

Two Hundred Million Animals

Imagine the two hundred million animals we kill for sport
each year. Imagine them piled in a heap – skulls,
beaks, horns, tusks, fangs, feathers, furs, scales, wattles,
coxcombs, paws, talons, flippers, bristles, tails.
Imagine their markings put asunder, their innards gauzed
by flies, their gassy sighs. Imagine them stuffed,
mounted, shrined. Ululate, then, the names we coin
to catch their beauty – we, who alone of all the creatures
have need of names, of categories, maybe
even of beauty, who laud their looks, the ways by which
they move, their temperament, their playfulness,
stealth and mystery – inspirations of art, music, poetry –
as though we would throw the earth open
before them, assert their inheritance the equal of our own.

Scribble Lark

How strange these lanes and hedgerows still
appear, making me want to look
deeper into them. The spider spinning a silk
sarcophagus about a wasp, tendering it
to a potential mate. The fern drawing on mist
to bless its fertilisation. The rat's burrow,
freshly earthed – but there's a wagtail
squatting in it now, having cosied the interior
with moss, a feisty little warrior
prepared to battle for hours, using the narrow
opening to hold the returned rodent off.
Sometimes I think I'm mad, leaning
past dusk, fascinated as the runny-nosed child
who long ago started the neighbours
wondering. My world is burning down, being
blown down, withering, drowning,
but on nights of deep freeze the wrens gather
as they have always done, a ball
of them rolled into one simply to keep warm,
while in spring the long-eared owl alights
on the spruce-tree nest accumulated by crows
and outsits their furore, or in another
scenario a yellowhammer warbles to his partner
the songs learned from his father
in the idiom and accent of this place; for here
is nature, working with its own will;
and here she sits – the 'scribble lark', hatching
a clutch of scribble-marked eggs, in
the rusted exhaust of an old tractor in a sawmill.

The Invisible Man

A teacup lifts, tilts, empties out of and into thin air
while he – bumped by an unsuspecting shoulder –
loses, recovers his composure. Present or absent, his bind
has us playing hide-and-seek. We see the wind
disfiguring his footprints on a sandy beach; the book
that floats, now open, now shut, before a run of bad luck
confirms him the victim of a flying fist, a knife
pressed towards its vanishing point, a handgun going off.
Blood dots the pavement. He appears to do
some good while we peer into our own futures, construe
skyscraper, subway, taxi cab, neon-lit come-hither,
wristwatch, popped-on sunglasses, near-fatal heart-flutter.
A city's run of the mill. After, a tranquil space –
clothes make him up; fedora and bandages define his face;
shirt, trouser legs fill out; a certain raffish élan.
Meanwhile, the open fire at our backs dies down;
we remember the draught under the door that's been there
all along, so stop walking in his lenient leather
shoes, fumble for the muddied farmyard boots that seem
no longer to fit us and, one at a time, twist into them.

Wild Barley

This spike with its brittle quiff or beard,
growing out of shingly ground
along the crooked lane behind our shed,
looks scuttish even as it seeds, looks
wayward as the graffiti sprayed
on garage walls in skeins of gold and red.

Sign of neglect, my neighbour says,
but when I pluck its green-tinged grains,
unhusk the measly kernels, place
them on my tongue, a chronicle teeters –
ancient, fundamental – which tastes
of rain and sunshine, the first stand our

ancestors made, the holding down
and raising up, with cricked backs, with
cracked fingers, of field and yield,
of all that would make for a city, its modes
and means, pomps and works,
from the scatter of primordial dunghills.

Houses

I doubted our flat-porch roof, where the sidling shadows
of the cypress trees at evening
goose-bumped me awake, could be half so marvellous
as the roofs of ancient Çatalhöyük,
which served as streets, had doors in them,
and ladders that led down into the houses. Each house

raised on the ruins of its predecessors a maker's space
for larder and fire, basket-weave
and bangle, mirror and dagger. Each as well
a burial chamber, bone-store of the ancestors, repository
of their preserved heads – kept,
much as we kept pisspots, under the beds.

No, the roomy house below me, draughty
and prone to creaks – with its wild-dog-rose wallpaper
peeling from the door jambs
that opened to the front and back yards, with cloud-flicker
across a ceiling or the sun's
pulsing aureole on chimney breast or floor –

couldn't hold a candle to Çatalhöyük's plaster-crafted
bulls' noggins and painted leopards.
But I valued height and flatness, the gift of a refuge where
nobody thought to look.
Things that were unremarkable then – a sewing machine
jangled into life by pressing on its treadle,

duck eggs submerged for coolness in a bucket of oats,
buttermilk left to clot in an enamel basin –
become strange enough, when I recount them, to puzzle

children today, just as the contents
of Çatalhöyük, in their prime
nine thousand years ago, still puzzle me. And the boy

on the roof, waking to wonders of his own nature
and place, follows in my footsteps as though to catch me up
with the harvest of mother images
he holds onto and the word he must travel by
even if destined to stay forever gone –
a father's 'never forget who you are, where you come from'.

The Migration

Once ever did I see the eels go on a belly march,
teems of them 'splathering' across the wet
Callows, homing to the seaweed of the Sargasso.

That must be when my neighbour poached them,
using a canvas bag – enough to keep him
fed for months. Thrown in a barrel, they coiled

and uncoiled in the run-off of rain from his roof,
under a heavy timber lid. Later,
in his cottage, I saw an eel jump from the frying pan

into a water bucket, a patch of unswept dust
displaced with a splash. He laughed,
slung the creature back in the pan. It sizzled,

it hopped and shrivelled and died hard. And then
he chopped and chewed it with a smile –
he, the 'frikener' of my boyhood, fulfilling his name.

But *eel*. The word made my head pulse
and reel, full of questing and full of the primordial
that couldn't be famished or argued down.

I wanted to follow the fairy-tale of the eels'
getaway through streams and rushes, over tar road
and clay path, shadow them as they glistened

by moonlight, in rain grew super-slicked,
shrank under the sun's bullying, were hoof-stamped
or even hawked up – their migration

yet unstoppable, so they would essay
towards the river mouths, read the jigsaw of the rocks,
play themselves undulant after toppling

off the land, voyage by a series of unwearying flexes
to spawn in the great gyre of the ocean.
I thought to trick the frikener, snare him

as Thanatos had been snared by Sisyphus
in a book. I saw the sad sack of himself, his struggles
rippling and wrinkling the hessian fabric,

swelling and slackening and standing it, suffering
its every collapse – bound, as a body is,
to live by tight confines, bump of heel to the cap

of the skull, poke of elbow and knee to the bunched
and knotted neck. I wanted, but the dream
was the doing and the heart would find another ache.

Poultice

A moth pinches and presses itself
in under the glass lampshade
attached to my hotel-room ceiling,
where it clicks and flutters
all evening, singed and stunned,
flaring out of its dying
to flap and flounder in the light.

I watch the fool's gold of its wings
collect as in a Petri dish
above my head, and feel how far
I fall short of wish fulfillment.
And miss the self-abandon
of the hurt boy delving fingers
into hives for solace not of honey

but of stings, or sleeping
under rough mercy of furze,
or diving in wells to cool the ardour
of nettles, pismires, sunburn.
And miss a reckless boy's
seeming attempts to maim himself,
before the sometime kindness

of the earth engendered his own.
No soft sentiment, no cure
but make do with slow mending.
So I haul up from nature's
messy heaven this poultice that settles
to a tingle, an afterglow,
a cornucopia of images huffed

off a spot-lit stage. Arc of hare, lift
of lark, marsh fritillary's
flit-with-breezes, each Callows river
running to loops that gathered
the waders – 'bog bleater',
'whaup' curlew, 'Goose of Ireland' –
to stitch the mud of little lakes.

They hold in mind – ageless,
busy, tranquil – silhouettes that switch
and shimmer at sunset;
as if their spectral cries, wing-wheels,
cheer-filled landings, had
brought me to imprint on them,
incline ever after towards waterland.

Fatherhood

Red-berried in spring, or pearled
with raindrops pale as winter daylight,
or bustled by bird or wind,
or shaken when wasps in autumn
scrounge its undersides
for living scraps, the cotoneaster
sends me back to a young man's climb –
up its arms along a shoulder
of wall; to the ivy overhang, which he
intends to prune and from where
he sees his infant daughter and son
standing near the kitchen door,
amazement on their faces
at his derring-do – and for a moment
he feels mawkish because he suspects
the garden won't stay rosy
forever but go the way of the leaves
he cuts or doesn't cut now,
the freshly budded haunts of squirrel
and wood pigeon he tries to keep
spry, all his fatherly care
grow frazzled or hard to say
no matter how fervently he holds to it;
so he shouts his love and acts
the clown – until they laugh, and wave,
and take off after the collie dog
chasing two white butterflies
on a close flit together silently tumbling.

Half-carcass of Calf

The frazzled white of fried egg bubbles up – but it is water,
polluted water at the edge of the lough.
I find a cockchafer dead among reeds, where the tide,
or what passes for a tide, trembles shallowly
across. Something wavers below the sun's glitter-making,

below the fried-egg scum – a half-carcass of calf,
the front half, raggedly sawn off. He hovers
one-dimensional – a mere sketch the blue staring eye, the pale
porcelain snout and yellow hoof. There,
in my bewildered boyhood, he speaks not in words

but through the appeal to emotion his truncated form
is still able to make – of life's lovely gambol
through Callows grass, of how barbarity shadows the loveliness
always, tricked up in the clotted primordial.
And because my mind runs ground-wise, or close,

I cannot help but picture an eel squirming
in a butterfly net after we dragged it from a bog hole,
a flame-furred cat tugged by its tail
back down our chimney once, the elasticity of a half-earthed
earthworm defying a robin – on and on

the stresses and strains of visions both repulsive
and beautiful. I gape out across the lough,
towards the peeping houses, the trees and haysheds, and whirl
with a wish to be as autonomous as the superhero
in a comic book, and the magic cloak

that is this circumstance of wet-meadow wilderness
spins as I spin – lost rivers and rare flowers
stitched in its raggy folds, turloughs coming and going, turloughs
and wild geese. I dip my hand, dreaming
an egg of blotched colour, a wolf spider with its pouch

of packed-up young, dreaming the spear-beaked skull
of a snipe, and as I trip, dizzying, the thick ooze
sinks under my nails, the torn scraw opens from knee to heel
a fast-flooding space, and in the disturbed
environs of the lough the half-carcass tilts and begins to rise.

Render

A 9ᵗʰ-century scribe considers the future of his manuscript

Somewhere in the hereafter, when my earthly life is over,
this black-leather psalter will crumble or burn,
or the pages become plastered together, the illuminated text
steeped in the muck of the mire, absorbing the stain
of bog myrtle and oak, seasoning until a hand or a shovel
or a slippage of the land turns it up. Psalm book,

prayer song, its dazzle of luminosities embezzles the sight
from my eyes; its swirl of ornate constructs
glosses vellum itch, quill scratch. I play trick-of-the-loop.
But even as I am tempted away from the rubric
of the monastery, from the blessings of rain and sunlight,
the crops my community stoop to raise to growth,

I dream the psalter tainted, and again I dream it elevated,
put to some fine settlement – in a workshop
where the care I take is lavished by methods I could never
concoct. Solvents cleverer than my own, gauges
and calculators faster than the human brain, the deep-seated
gaze of future apparatuses – will these fathom

how letters might have shrunk or stretched, gone cracked
or hotchpotched, the job at its plainest rendered
to a raggy beast's pelt? And conspire to make it pristine
once more? But woe, the cat I keep – to keep me guessing –
leapt today out of thin air, and I could only roar
in helpless high dudgeon to see him paw-printing the script.

I maunder, the images in their flare and stare
making me dizzy until I forget myself and see a stranger
leaning, maybe centuries from now, able to spot
the ink-smudge where the cat padded, to imagine the hail
of curses cuffing his white tail, to picture us both,
Pangur and man, one scattering, the other's thunder stolen.

The Soldier on Clare Island

Later we will picture U-boat torpedoes skeeting water,
shattering a ship's keel, rupturing its hull.
And imagine him flipped into the air, flopped
backwards, explosions splashing the various distances –
shards of hissing metal, limbs of men, bales,

boxes, bags and barrels enough to tide Noah's ark
over the deluge. And dream of fishes
weaving in and out of his wounds, slick as needles
threading stitches through mounds
of cloth draped across our nanas' thighs. In games

and quiet reflections he will live on, he will move
again – the dead soldier, ocean currents
spinning him towards us by trouser cuff or coat lapel,
sousing his ear, braiding seaweed in his hair.
But the day he arrives, nudging against the rocks,

all we can do is shrink to the reticence
our parents and neighbours wear as a way of life,
the set notions of dignity they expect
from us. He floats, so much a sodden garment
we are unsure at first whether there is a body or not.

A fisherman's hands gather him up
where we stoop, short-trousered, splay-toed. The sea
relinquishes its grip in surly rivulets emptying.
His face, sky-lit but dull, gives him away.
His uniform, once remarked on, seems no longer

to fit him. An Englishman – the grizzled heads nod –
he must be Protestant, so. Their words
perturb us out of our welling pity. No name found,
no place to send him home to, measures
taken for a decent burial, a graveyard of his own

beyond the shoulder of our Catholic cemetery.
War thunders elsewhere. Echoes reach us, 'dispatches'
from either side neutrally reported, and he,
a casualty spat by the long-drawn Battle of the Atlantic,
is considered part of 'a necessary detriment'.

But if strafings we suffer seem slight by comparison,
storm and tidal swell still cut us off; we feel
the pang of infant deaths, of kinfolk
exiled, of famine remembered around smoky turf fires
or forebears grieved as we stare at the lazy-bed

residues of old potato ridges skeletally stretched.
Wonders happen regardless, nature
requiring only itself. Birds sing the rinsed air and light,
spider webs glisten on spars of gates,
tadpoles tickle the ribs of streamlets and loughs.

But what the soldier might give to see a rainbow
spanning the cove, or a school of basking sharks
swimming nose-to-tail just offshore,
or sunlight shimmering a waterlogged *fulacht fiadh*,
has faded with him. As for arguing the world

or its wear, or whether the heather painting the hills
is red or purple, orange or green,
we doubt such matters would cost him a thought
if he could live his life over. One house
owns a wireless, and with the 'big people' gathered

to hear far-off, bellicose, defiant voices, we climb
the forbidden graveyard wall, embed spikes of foxglove,
'dead man's fingers', where we tread,
supposing the soldier's feet, supposing his head.
And climb again when we are older:

courting couples wanting privacy, wanting to feel
our bodies eased away; find ourselves
led – after we bundle and kiss – to recollect him sunken
in the clay-covered dark, to imagine a love
of his own and how maybe she waits, still waits,

the war ten years ended. Ten years, ten more,
the grist of decades anchors and layers us. The wall
stands, and beyond it other walls, each
a front for something – peace, prayer, commemoration,
even the notion that the dead, if permitted

to mingle, might twist, as the living do, old grievance
into fresh feud. He lingers, almost a fiction,
yet niggling us until we must clear the 'buttermilk' moss
that smothers his bed. Hold a ceremony,
someone says, find and invite his relatives, but first

knock down the dividing wall. Our shoes bruise
the damp hillside grass. Politicians and military men extol
the soldier's sacrifice. An orphan, we hear, born
in Wales; kind, helpful, quick with a joke.
And – the speaker smiles, clears his throat – a Catholic.

2

A Fable

Beside Lake Tonle Sap, two mahouts
and their two elephants.
The mahouts chat quietly in a language
related to Khmer, before speaking
each to his elephant
in a language of his own creation.
Each elephant nods,
seeming to know what is meant.
Then one mahout tells the other a story
about two elephants
carrying two mahouts through the water,
about a frog that jumps up
onto one elephant's ear,
and clings there. The elephant's rider
reaches to grab the frog,
intending to cook it later for dinner,
but his friend says,
we dare not disturb it; let it travel
in safety with us: it means
the world to me – it means the elephant.

Esther

Esther's days grew into a pattern. Her moments
made stitches. And there it was, the fabric
of her life. If certain stitches had fantastic names,
or called up places far removed – the Breton,
the Bosnian, the Algerian eye stitch –
from the plain wooden bench she worked at

in the Magdalen laundry, she found the darns still
could trick smoothly between her fingers
but that in the shading of one thread with another
lived the more complex body of the matter.
Sometimes, she would feather-stitch, loop to right
and left off a stem or a shoot, and this

lead to flowers. Then there were the knots –
Antwerp edging stitch, French knot,
Chinese 'forbidden' stitch – and moments caught
all in one long moment twisted about the needle
she passed through and across her quiet
breathing, the silent story swaddled next her heart.

Esther's embroideries reached the high street shops
of London. Her own drab, unadorned clothes,
her docked hair, the lack of possessions
that was her lot, promoted, according to the Sisters,
modest conduct, pounds she brought in
held to elevate their prayer, ask pardon for her sin.

My Mother's Getaway

'Aren't we lucky to have them?'
She meant the walking places,
her own wildering realm. No meals
to cook, no groceries to fetch,
no cows to milk, no cattle to herd
or sheep to flock. Danger?
There were only shallow drains
and slack fences to step,
with a hitch of her skirt, across.
Yes, 'across' – depend on her
to say that word. She'd go across
the Callows, face Aughty's
distant blue hills forecasting
fine weather, or face near-at-hand
Aughty's glum readiness
to add to the splosh of rust-red
ferric iron water in the field
known as Old Tillage. No walls
or trees for 'a quare hawk'
to hide behind, the land flat, her eyes
able to see far. She'd go
morning or evening to the nurture
of not thinking, her feet swishing
through coarse meadow –
go across, away from child and beast
and man, go beyond concern.

Amcotts Moor Woman

Everything breathed. I planted my bare feet each in turn
and felt the shoemaker tuck and fold the cured
cowhide ankle-deep about them, cutting and stitching
with a peep for the toes and the straps
curling unbroken extensions. Run a tug-tassel off the top

of the heel, I told him – it happened so long ago that he
would surely gasp if handed the proof
of 'his' shoe, crafted to endure, enduring 'so well'. Where,
he might ask with half a laugh, is the other sandal?
Weren't they a match, the missing one well-made as this?

A frown might crease his face and his fingers
grease his brow as he tried to recall the woman who bought
the 'dainty pair of kicks' from him. Or would he
blink tears at the thought of the woman's
'disappearance'; or coldly look away, unwilling to meet

your gaze; or even rant – he, who seemed gentle-natured –
about 'her sort' deserving what she got?
And you, eyeing the thin moccasin that lingers, try to picture
my wander over Amcotts Moor, how I skited
through sphagnum and heather, the weeps and deeps

no earthly trouble, with bog cotton – the hovering ghost
of summer – a ready stoop and pick. Guess me fresh-faced
if you will, guess me dark or fair, gathering
the white eggs of a bird that nests in a hole in the ground,
or picking bilberries; guess me flowing in silk,

or with chapped lips grimacing at life's skimps and hardships.
Or do I sing because being most able
to hear myself when walking alone? A day inhabited
by ordinary deeds – but now, suddenly, figure me hurrying,
taken, battered and broken. Or maybe I drown,

or simply forget my way, who slip – however it happens –
to the dream you've yet to meet, cold paralysis
in its kiss and clay its consumptive grip. The shoe survives.
It stays even after my body, so long hidden
by the mire, is found and lost again, frittered on the journey.

Here, snug-fit for my left foot, tawny and delicate-looking
as a wild mushroom, it waits, and might wait
forever if you ask that of it, with the soft shadow of the mouth
exposed to your every conjecture even as
it asserts the irretrievable, silently, inside a casket of glass.

Towards a Frontier

1.

Our feet are rude. They endure. Our hearts are set
on living through what we suffer.

On a journey that takes so long we lose track
of its beginning, of how a dream of freedom becomes
a sorry dance.

2.

　　　　　We grind as we move.

'Round wind', 'ghost's wind', 'sand devil' –
these swirling pillars
we receive by different names, depending on where

we come from.

3.

　　　　　Our children suck stones.
Our hands miss the boat, or when
we are at last afloat,
the thing sunders under us – we thrash and fail;
our bodies swell with water.

4.

> Here, an innocent,
> washed up for the world to mull over. There, a village,
>
> smoking the heavens, a tyrant
> smiling as he dines on our weeping flesh.
>
> Beyond us, stumbling, others go, towards a frontier.

Boxes

The rustle of mouse / The stink of fox / The thump of rain...

I read these phrases on a box in which your art materials
were brought, haltingly
as I once read the fog-breath of a cow –
it stuck to a parlour window
while the cow herself stood outside, hidden by the night.

Natural phenomena, preferably inexplicable,
spur me when I write, such as balls of lightning that spin
and float, now fast, now slow, now up,
now down, as if possessed
of a mind of their own, able to push against a storm, pass
through concrete or glass,
leaving only a rotten-eggs whiff –
and sometimes death – should they go off.

Airline pilots and submariners from their austere stations
report just such radiant spheres
emerging clean through iron,
circumventing or seeming to circumvent immutable laws.

So wonder again becomes the child of some
unfathomed thing. And once,
when she was young and a storm was blowing, my sister
saw a blue-gold, buoyant moon
that seemed to stare at her before cresting the pinnacles
of the cypress trees and vanishing.

Her haunting haunts me still,
just as the cow's breath wraithed on the windowpane
will, or the husky laugh,
with mockery in it, sometimes chucked
from a breezy sky by a seagull, or the sight of the rufous fox
stepping, vertical, deliberate,
across our old sheepdog's grassy grave in moonlight.

But what about *The rustle of* ... ?
I propose a stranger, maybe a poet from another language
or place, wrestling with altered life,
exiled circumstance,
in a warehouse, say, on box after cardboard box – scratch
of a marker, its fumes
making for a headache by the time lunch break is over.

And the boxes dispatched, each to
an artist, and each artist embarked on his or her creation.

Renoir

One stifled groan, the old boy rises
from his wheelchair, takes
a shaky step out onto the veranda.
His cotton shift, breeze-blown,
shows the cleft of his bony haunches;
his heels appear to bruise
the tiles that bruise them, and then
he's there, framed by wood,
grumbling about something – maybe
his crocked bones or the colours
that have slipped his palette,
or how he doesn't care what happens
so long as he can still paint –
he's there, or nearly, one dying dip,
one dab of the art-ravened
corpus, no fun felt in flesh anymore,
and, as he goes forward into
the light of day, he grows translucent.

Contesting Cuckoos

Sumer is icumen in and I feel as if I've been living here
forever, the landscape wild as when the old
song cheering on the cuckoo was first written down,

or as if I've slipped into the sandals of that cantor
of the 13th century, his Wessex dialect – or he into mine.
Lhude sing, cuccu; let me accompany you.

Groweth sed and bloweth med – is that how the words go? –
and springth the wode nu. Hearty countryman,
I hear you. *Sing, cuccu!* – a few miles away to the west.

No dither or doubt, *Bulluc sterteth, Bucke
uerteth,* play it out. *Ne swic thu naver nu.* The more so
as, eager to outdo you now, a rival starts up

through the moonlit mist. The battle rolls to and fro, neck
of the wood to neck of the wood, then a lull,
a spellbound interlude; and still the living multitudes

gather and grow, the huge and heedless compulsion
of nature towards its accomplishment holds true.
Sing, cuccu, nu; sing, cuccu; Sing, cuccu; sing, cuccu, nu!

Cleft in Metal

The wren's headache is to get her little brood
out alive. Out of a cleft in the band-saw's metal jaw,
away beyond the saw-teeth's seething spin.

Somehow the trembling colossus holds, one
stay-put centimetre short of smithereening the nest
and doddle of chicks within. Not that she

went in with her eyes shut. Depended on instinct's
given spec, worked her head to calibrate
angle and arc, due no extra credit – yet we admire

the adroit flit around a blade, the lining
of twiglets with moss, wool, even with rabbit's fur
and wood shavings collected by her mate.

Finally, she put a gloss to everything in the shape
of brown-speckled eggs, judged these
would live deaf to noise, settled against the hubbub.

It was as if a switch had been pressed –
her stillness, and, under the velvety breast feathers,
secret runnels and scurries of incubating yolk

finding the right spots, ramps and revs of the much
to do with machine, the more that is apart:
goo coagulations and the mystery pounding a heart.

Budgerigar

The bay window's net curtains are what we notice first,
their faded, sand-yellow look suggesting a tide
has gone out. Then the tendrils of scrubland grass – as near
to your native habitat as we can get – climbing
the white grid of your cage. Nature programmes on TV
you will answer with a chirrup, or the robin
that comes with morning to the sill, a cross-fertilisation
trying to happen, a tantalising trade-off in song.
But rock music is your favourite, its rhythms 'stomping'
your twig feet, its screech excoriating the world
through your open throat. You don't grow to resemble us,
to appear grateful or to regret. We seem nothing
you could cherish or be improved by, or wish
to cuddle up to in your doubtful role as family pet. Are we
cold-hearted, caging you? Ah, there's a place
we have no wish to go; you occupy one small compartment
in our busy heads that – if it occurs to us – we evade
by means of the make-believe beach beyond
the curtains, the wilderness down-sized to a potted plant.

The tree growing inside a man's lung

is smaller than a bonsai, with its roots the thinnest
of threads taking to the lung's
alveoli, though whether each drawing of breath
causes it to tremble or swell, as might
a breeze quivering common or garden canopies,
we cannot tell, but it does grow –
an accredited five centimetres from the wet-warm
aerated 'earth' constricting the man's chest,
racking him as he tries to cough phlegm.
A shock, then, to the doctors when they examine
the x-rays he has undergone,
a variation on the notion of daisies being pushed up
by a buried corpse. Still, things play host
to things. Nature – pliable, porous –
feasts off itself. And in this instance all ends well,
the little fir tree 'felled', the man
able, should he so decide, to make a keepsake of it
in a wallet or a locket, to smile at the looks
on friends' faces, to breathe freely
for the first time in ages as he propagates the tale.

The Pull

There was a distance to run, where the sliotar ran,
between Curnán and another young man.
The pull happened there. Be first, or simultaneous,
or suffer the coward's scar. Curnán, son
of the king of Connaught, was first. His hurley

swung, striking the sliotar, striking as well the head
of his opponent, who died of the injury.
This story came to me courtesy of an old hurler
who might himself have been Oisin
fallen from the horse, so withered and woebegone

he trembled as we stood in the rain at a bus-stop
on Stannaway Road, a drop of mucus
dangling from his nose. What little
could I say to deny or approve, other than that one
of the first hurling matches of modern times

was held at nearby Crumlin Common? Yet he flew
into high commentary on hearing this –
it's what we live for, he shouted, hurling continuity,
and he threw shapes through remembered deeds
of wristy men, and recited the names

of parishes, Cushendall to Blackpool by way of Birr,
Oulart, Carrickshock, Toomevara, Castlegar,
while traffic squeeged by on the rain-pelted tarmac
and two schoolboys looking sideways up
at him moved their mouths and hands in silent mimicry.

Shiners

We shone wood – dressers, hurley sticks, spade handles,
even coffin lids – until the sandpaper reddened
and buffed our palms. When an emery belt was installed,
we pressed the timber against it and gladdened
at the sibilance, and felt the ticklish dust whiten our brows,
and our minds grow weightless. Behind us,
unimaginably far, we reckoned a long line of shiners
making their own improvements, seeds or crushed grass
used as the first scrubbers, rough horsetail plant,
seashell, sharkskin found to polish things off. Elbow grease
a given, with always someone thinking to invent;
agents, agencies – the way the world goes, the way it went,
back through the forgotten, to the living fossil,
coelacanth, smoothing through dint of its abrasive scales.

The Wedge

Mid-morning winter wood, he turned from felling a tree,
threw the 5 lb. steel wedge and the sledge
aside, set a fire of stooked twiglets and dry tufts of moss
in a clearing, boiled a kettle and wet the tea.
The sledge has lost its handle; the thick end of the wedge –
dull despite its glint – still wears the blows
he sweated over at Ballydoogan, Coole Park and Myode,
as snaggle-teeth. Its thin end's a jagged line;
plain dent of splitting. And though I dream there's a door
somewhere that shows his way with wood,
or a floor that goes floating back half a century and more
to carpenter heaven – even see him at a bench within,
sawing timber with the sawdust flying – here,
this side of the sever, the wedge leaves me none the wiser.

Undercut

The shock rebounded off the trunk. Sometimes
the axe got stuck, had to be jiggled,
squeaked loose. Again you would lift and swing,
chips whizzing as you followed the tree

around, chopping until it grew thin, its raggy beak
resembling the nib of a huge, badly pared pencil.
Everything – branch and leaf, lizard
and moth, bird and nest of birds, even the clouds

in their constant shape-shift – appeared
to balance on or about that bole; the very air helped
to keep it aloft, dressed in grace
despite its colossal downward press. The pencil,

as image and as instrument, has stayed with you
since. To use it is to travel back
to the beginning, to an old oak desk, your face
focused and fierce, your forearm uncreasing a page,

each letter found to topple forward
as though the prevailing westerlies had pushed it,
the pencil's velvety 'lead' point smudging
your tongue as you deliberated. Word fed word,

images sprouted, sentences were shaped. Again
you walked the woods, swung the axe
and scanned the canopy quaking above your head.
A secret 'mind what you're doing' voice,

a creaking sound – the undercut snapped, the tree
fell with a rending crash, a miserable bounce.
The solid uses to which timber can be put
happened now. But poems as a means of retrieval,

though they seemed only the ghosts
of all that was won and lost in that suddenly cleared
space – these drew you away, the plain
light of day slanting in to occupy a changed terrain.

3

The Refuse Gatherers

Underfoot there is nothing new, only litter's slow
reversion to muck – a bread wrapper,
a chocolate box, a coke can – all the garish slogans
wearing thin, with print ink and photo

plastering a wet pavement. We sweep the leaves
into a truck, take them to the wood
and give them back. Draw breath beside the Dodder,
our thoughts following the source and course

of forgetfulness proposed by the river,
our histories and griefs lulled where we gaze at weir
or waterfall, the torrent's frothy race
over stick-and-pebble installations – bird figures,

bare-domed Buddha men left by artists
to some toppling end. Grey-lit in the glittery shallows,
a heron: stooped motionless. Suddenly
she plunges, all neck and beak, provoking a splash.

The waggling tail is held aloft, adjusted;
the head swallowed first. Then, just as she stretches
to a squawky take-off, panicked words
burst from our cab radio: somewhere a bomb,

a shooting, the thin skin of civilisation
ruptured again, the sprawl of fresh atrocities let crawl.
We square our shoulders, push through
the automatic nature of each task; the heron's guzzle;

the mind by which people moseying
along a pavement are broken and torn – these happen

over in our thoughts. And, with them,
old remembrances we can't seem to get past:

a child sinking into the steaming gullet of a side-street
in Bucharest, a cardboard box ripped open
of a morning in Dublin – the sheeting
rain, the softening frost – to reveal a perished vagrant.

Between

The man in his coffin in the funeral home,
and the man in a mechanised cab
guiding the jib of a crane above the street,
divide my afternoon between them –

I linger at the mortuary door, enter and edge
back out, remembering a line
written by the dead poet, appraising the height
the crane driver sits at, turn again

where the framed, unsmiling photograph
next the coffin's foot shows a back-packer
hard-hoofing through hill country,
wreathed in sweat and sunlight. I knew him

neither in sickness nor health, knew
only that he struck for innovation in his work,
sought to sunder the personal,
bury the lyric, scream the gaps in living –

but there's no fret left now, only the calm
it seems safe to say the dead know.
I lift on my own steam, on the shaky fulcrum
of my bones, reclaim the grinding noise,

scan the rain-glistened rooftops,
the windows the crane man can see down into
from his Plexiglass and steel eyrie.
And maybe this one dreams he is God

swinging the city – piecemeal, geometric – up
and over, singing the less bother

of old times, simpler organisms, when life
was a pottage sluggishly simmering,

or archaeopteryx or pterodactyl flapped along
with no thought of moral conundrum,
of prayer or petition. Or maybe he has eyes
only for what he must follow through,

the new block rising above restaurant
and shoe shop, while at street level I watch cars
throttle for the hills beyond Rathfarnham,
a crow's pantaloons flensed by the wind

as she pirouettes, wings aloft, on the heads
of traffic lights, a dog jostle his walker
as they go – and there, the coffin,
here the tower crane penduluming to and fro.

Manhole Cover

Cast in the foundry of Tonge & Taggart, 1909 –
of all whose weight it has taken
since, the only evidence now is a dull shimmer,
a trace of wear and tear
tempering the studded iron's face. Say

we are more than ghosts
gliding over. Say what fine accommodations
our feet arrive at in their deliberations
with metal and concrete,
even as they miss the give of grass.

Let steam engines rumbling through our skulls –
flanged wheels revolve
the reds and rusts of a childhood
we claim as our very own
even if it never held such ballast – bring us round

to consideration of manhole covers.
O life of nature skipped
and skimmed, each journey aimless unless
accomplished in the lingering.
I drag my heel, each time I pass, against the abyss.

Disappearing Acts – A Street Triptych

1.

Excuse me, Sir, the raggedy man says, but is it morning
or evening? It's midnight, I tell him, and the way
he swings, bottle tucked underarm, back
towards the bushes, reminds me of how birds stop singing
during a solar eclipse, or spiders build again
after rain has sundered their webs. The brown ruddiness
of his broad, bewhiskered face, his draggled coat
and stumbling gait – the shine of a streetlamp
through branches accentuates the blue bruise of his lips,
the glisten where his eyes are concerned.
But what do I know of travails steeped and seared
into him – the endless nowhere of his waiting, the fuddled
stimuli of light and dark, the dragged-out
disappearing act of his life as he heads for an early end?
Conscience, there's a thing. Fine words
follow me home, fine words and my failure to take him in.

2.

Your fleece-jacket's tattered, drenched through to the lining.
Sleeplessness and sedation make you stagger,
slur your words. The hospital security men, posturing
their paraphernalia – walkie-talkies and waist-wrist
restraints – chat quietly together, tap the sides of their skulls.
I come to this first-hand, your thin body
stared into submission, sentenced to a padded room with one
tiny window where the hours won't change your mind.
At daybreak they let you go, no bed to spare,
no remedy found. You wander and wait,

your gentleness countenanced a crime, your talent, twist
of difference, meted only scorn. And if yesterday
my melancholy was van Gogh's letters to art and brotherhood,
the painter's word cleanly put, his passionate
heart poured out, today I pray comfort find you
who shiver – otherwhere, far – on the frayed edge of a street.

3.

The wind rises; the cherry tree beyond the church window
blusters and bluffs, flickers and flurries as if to show
you are dancing still, throwing shapes as off
down the motorway you go, shining in our reverie, clowning
amid squalor and squall, rattling gates, scutting
on the backs of lorries. The world mutters that you failed
even as a petty criminal, your few scrapes with the law
veering more towards hilarity than thievery in small
newsprint, your ear-ring and tattoos, your fast-faded promise
as a footballer, let linger in sad, stereotypical remarks.
But we who make omens of ordinary things,
who see the wind as a ghost, say every space you lay claim to
becomes you, all creation is yours to pass through.
You've got out, gone out; by your own hand you've done this.
Here, delusion fails us. We slip from dreaming
a parallel universe where you at last come home to yourself.

Starlings

Bell sound, but not a call to worship or celebration,
and with no rattle of alarm running along it,
only a low drone which draws me on
against the breeze, through the late evening streets
of this sleepy, rust-tinted Tuscan hill town,
until I reach a small, stand-alone tower
centuries old and begun to crumble, the bell within
seeming to mingle a murmur with a snore.
Then starlings – a few flitting, the rest
tucked up tight together, the base of the campanile
smitten lime-white with their waste.
I want to linger, for in the deepening darkness I feel
as if all the lives become one creature,
and that the last bell to toll will be the bell of nature.

Anthony of the Desert

Nowhere to whit my dull and lazy self, my boredom
down to size, but this wilderness of broiling sun
and sandstorm lash. I straighten to clarify mirages
shimmering towards the horizon, bleached
bones of camel lying half-submerged a little distance

uphill, and in my slipshod sandals my bitten toes
weep blood as I trudge on – a stumblebum in the eyes
of the citizens of Crocodilopolis, worshippers
of the bejewelled reptile. Horned viper and scorpion
pester; primal devils threaten and tempt me

through the long dark's starry shiver. I find a tomb
to dwell in, drag the flat slab over, occlude
the world in tenacious dying while yet made to weave
prayer and palm leaf amid the saltbush beard
and dandruff of God. But soon again leprous limbs

come shambling and scraping; wretched faces
drip sweat, drip dusty mucus. 'You who know the soul
of nature,' they plead, 'tell us the nature
of the soul.' It doesn't matter how far I retreat,
or into what stony hole. They close on me,

silly saint-seekers, discommoded emissaries of empire,
and the broken poor for whom I most hold love.
Readying – it never feels odd – I drink the surly water
as God's given piss, eat the desiccated loaf
of misery he bakes, embrace his dune-drifting solitude.

North Mayo Haiku

Our latest clearing –
Nephin keeping its distance
travels with us still.

Wild roses, raindrops;
each stone quarry stands open
to blossom and fall.

A ditched toilet bowl,
a streamlet flowing through it
high on Sralagagh.

Fern and celandine,
a mattress printing its own
celandine and fern.

All the sun-shot geese
falling now on Annagh Marsh –
a child's flamingos.

A picnic's leavings
around Rathlacken court tomb,
the bog closing in.

Torso

He looks made of frog skin, darker than harvest frog, the span
of his arms imaginable in perches, his shut fists
clutching heather, squeeging gloops of sphagnum as he sits
propped, the head gone missing – screamed off,
you might say, into common decay, and with it his last pleas,
his unmerciful agonies. But if so raggedly truncated,
the torso floats centuries deep under bog's wet blanket, spits
of tannic acid conspiring to keep it. Stabbings happen,
breast-sleáned ingots, sour-puss holes where eels
and bicycle tyres linger and a TV set not quite able to drown
eyeballs the heavens. Now what big child or little king
refuses, through his long death as through his short life, to toe
the line, what horror, what wrong of ours is fessed up
in this sorry, welted scrappage of the sad old son of Croghan?

Roaming Maamtrasna

It sends him back, reading lichens by the edge of the lough,
to the first fine filaments of frost he saw
patterning a bedroom window. 'Loch na Fuaiche', named
for the winnowing winds, has him thinking
of how sight dims and wild places
grow less, has him savouring still the chill air as he blends
with grey-wraithed clouds and primordial
tree-stumps, as he puts words to nature that it neither needs
nor heeds. World promised this: the end
found even at the beginning, in a ram's crooked horn
lodged among lilies, in a ram's bleached and skeletal noggin,
its crevices stained with moss – empty,
for all that, of what passed for a ram's thoughts;
and the sensation of his own skull always ripe for plucking.

T. Rex Skull, Ulster Museum

Dinosaur fossils in glass cases, genuine articles
from Antrim's coast, lead us where this skull,
no direct relation of theirs, looms out of low light
among the museum dead, its huge
snaggle-teeth grinning. A small boy stares
open-mouthed, maybe wishing that he could hug
for comfort the polka-dotted toy dragon
propped beside his own bed, while the mind
of his grandfather, who stands beside him,
retrieves a horse's saddle – sweated and chafed –
from a musty stable. But whether God
backtracked, or nature – so full of funning –
pooh-poohed, or a chance meteor
put the Cretaceous sunlight and its creatures out,
we find illustrated here what the 'tyrant lizard'
could do: kill, devour, get rid. And agree
that this sombre convolution of bones – jawline,
eye-socket, seat of the brain – makes
the ancient ground-shaker 'real' again, the legend
tangible and new. A sense of fellow feeling
softens the awe engendered in us, yet
at back of our throats some deep-seated thing
which we can't dismiss as vestigial
subsists, holding ready to erupt – the cuff of fierce
proclivities, capable still of striking home:
dire deeds, dread devices to carry them through.

A Stopped Moment in Childhood

The house and garden, the hay-stack and wallside roses,
stood all within my sights as I revolved slowly
on the linchpin of a new power – weightless, levitational –
with gun-barrel eye and the mahogany stock
nibbling at my shoulder. Admiration for the clean lines
of metal and wood beamed itself back at me
in my shaping to be somebody with whom only a fool
would trifle. The Scots pine in the ash pit
transformed to cactus, the rusted barn missing a few sheets
of galvanise became a canyon in this western
sustained by my training the rifle. Decisiveness,
derring-do – and a potential subtraction from everything.
But what might take my trigger-finger's fancy,
what get in the way? Robin flitting twig to twig? Magpie
on the footpath hopping nearer? Because, holding
the gun so and feeling the fierce, aimed faces
of my companions on me, I knew I was expected to fire.

The Victor

The ghost of de Ginkell, the victor, rode towards me
on the way to Kiltulla while I took shelter
from a sudden summer squall under a huge ash tree
that might have been the son or daughter
of the ash tree which long ago had been named after him.
As I watched, rain through the leafy canopy
dripped, seeming to whisper the blood of Aughrim's
battle-dead. Quietly he passed, and quietly
his cavalry followed; I couldn't tell if there was sorrow
on the faces, or the least spasm of joy, yet heard
flintlocks rattle, saw bannered crosses blow
above wide-brimmed hats; then the hoof-clops wavered
and everything lapsed – so my dream insists –
following the lie of the land, into distance, into mists.

Achilles Regrets

This glorified cave – more dungeon
than distinction of shades –
I wander, missing the sunshine,

missing the stars and the stone pines
flung against them wavering
in the wind, missing the thousand

trembles of life, its attendant
irritations of which I once so happily
complained. Echoes come down –

of my renown as a soldier,
the bravery that cost me, yet there
where the colours dance

and the sounds still ring, they love me
most for dying young.
I'm your guitar man fixed forever

in a rock and roll idyll
after he OD's at the height of his glory,
your prize fighter who takes

one too many punches to the skull.
Or – depending on where
allegiances lie – the terrorist

who blows himself and other people
up, the freedom fighter
extolled by this or that land

or band. I find no purpose
in over-lordship of the breathless dead.
The real world happens above

my head, the power-monger's croon,
the hungry pleading for bread,
and – too often for comfort –

a politician's swell sentiments woven
from the grief of strangers
in order to amplify a lily-livered tune.

Till the Next Time

i.m. Robert May, died WW1, June 1916

'God might…' he wrote, by way of ending his letter
from the trenches, but any thought he held
of saying more to his friend, your grandfather,
stopped, the shell upsetting everything
in his vicinity, the pages blown free by the blast,
and with them his 'Thanks for the razor,
it is a good one'; his 'Sorry to hear about Tony,
such things will happen' – war or death
not otherwise referenced; his 'I have said all till
the next time' left hanging as he is tossed
into the air, a few drops of his blood splashed against
the floating white space he must have looked
hard at for a moment before deciding
to settle on the beginning of a hope or a blessing.

4

Precursor

Tetrapod hardly covers it, old boy or girl
climbing out of the sea.
Tetrapod, four-foot, accurate but basic

as the mud in my mind's eye
you are plodding. Amphibian then, since
you take a fresh element,

the shelf of land, cumbersomely on,
all to do in your warted skin.
Newt might fit, or giant newt, as you lay

down a trackway of footprints
that – once fossilised – will size you up,
a metre in length from snout

to tip of frill-fringed tail. Behind you
the sound of breaking waves
we may, even at this remove, construe

as lonesome, or evoke pathos
by describing how surfs erode residual
drag-marks of the tail itself,

or imagine you in your stolid progression
busy still, flicking the air
with your tongue, tasting its potential.

Then you've gone, wisps of dust covering
all trace, slow petrifaction
come to pass, shift of tectonic plates

shaping seas and landmasses
until – a mild breeze, a sunny morning –
there's us boarding the ferry

to Valentia Island, to the spot where
someone's naming of you
as the world's first land-animal is traceable

as a little fossilised amble,
and though this ends abruptly where
a cleft in rock strikes water, still we dance

and dabble our feet
in the shallow streamlet that slides
across, linking and fructifying everything.

Toad

Warted as maybe a witch is, or 'ugly and venomous'
according to the exiled Duke in *As You Like It*,
or a metaphor for the cold, squatting thing felt to exist,
Philip Larkin's poem asserts, both outside
and inside a life – you yet carry your robust self,
your cladding of lichened colours, back far
before us, to the epoch of dinosaurs. Snibs of rock,
effervesces of air trapped in ancient ice, fossils
and other artefacts – these help unlock primal secrets.
But if I suggest I can discern behind your eyes
sights your ancestors may well have seen –
of horrendous *Hatzegopteryx*, for example, crouched
under tarpaulin of leathery wing-webbing,
or juddering its head as it swallows a smaller animal;
or if in my enthusiasm I credit you contain,
buried deep inside your brain, no gemstone or antidote
to poison, but a residual spectre of terror,
the comet blast of impact winter that all but finished
everything – well, this skew-whiff song I offer
cherishes, still, your muddling through, your survival.

Seals Conversing

Sounds the grey seals utter now – *yah-*
nuuuh, hy-awk, noo-eh-whoo –
from the rocky islet, filling, forsaking
your ear, haunt you more
because themselves haunted, full
of wobble, amplified by cave,
awaking chatter you once were party to
under a breathy chimney,
echo, echolalia, beginning of things,
the aches simple then,
but tonight you yearn, you quail
before the mesh and mow
of unanswerables even as the sea
in its hugeness sets the seals conversing
out where salt air ventriloquizes,
no sirens singing, still a spell
rises so much in keeping with your
feeling for the improbable
or peculiar that you muster up your own
spine-tingling creature –
full-throated, able to bear – which
through a lull in the swoosh
or sough offers its *awk-so, eh-whoo, hy-no,*
ya-nuuuh, catching and cradling
the vocables of mother
to cub, cub to mother, and it is enough
for you, this word of shelter,
of fishing grounds or what's in the air.

North Mayo Night

The 'rowboat' moon rears up on its prow
as though it has caught the swell
of the sea-blue sky. Dún Briste gives itself
away by the frothy whiteness I see

lapping at its base, while a jet slips, sparkle
after ruby sparkle, towards America,
and a star too bright to be a star ogles me.
The streetlights of Ballycastle shine,

the smell of a day that's done and dusted
hangs in the heather and on the air,
an unseasonably hot day in April
spent strolling the hills of Sralagagh. Lucky

to have lived, to be alive – is this
too blithe a thing to say? Not when I feel
lifted to rapture I can account for
only by the heady furze, the drowse of crows

silent at last in their rookery
become my pleasure here, the wear of sad
seasons and storm-scattered shapes
twigged to life, stirred to nurture once more.

It's a passing spell, our resonance
and room; the world finds ways to fail us all.
Still I recall 'rowboat', 'galleon' –
old words penned by an old poet long cast

adrift on the mainsail of his vessel,
in my fashion follow the push of the moon

through the bulked and blackened
addendum of the roosts, to break the gloom.

The Boat

It serves as an umbrella, the boat on top of a tree,
only the odd drip coming through, all
that furious rain song playing *for* rather than *on* us
as we squint at the watery-eyed pinholes
in our aluminium ceiling. And when the downpour
stops, we still linger even if our thoughts
are ferried away to dwell on such tall tales
as the 'unearthing of Noah's Ark' on Mount Ararat,
or the stone seat that 'floats' in our local
park, its four legs submerged under an inundation
from the River Dodder. The world
that works to mismatch things, that has them
play off one another – we live for this,
our own out-of-kilter nature approved by the boat's
resemblance to a hammerhead shark
as it tilts above us here; in the returning sunshine's
pale, slantwise beams found to waver
at each drag and jig of the upturned vessel
on a rig of branches breasting the ocean of the air.

Downpatrick Head

Blowholes snuffle; spray shoots up through grids
we set across them for our protection.
And maybe Crom Dubh, the pagan chieftain, still
skulks on the Rock of Duross promontory,

out by the edge of the cliff while St. Patrick
tries to convert him. We catch them
arguing in the language of the wind, howling curses
back and forth, or imagine we do, for this

is the myth and the myth feels more real here
than elsewhere, whittles disbelief until
you see the saint pound his crozier
in exasperation, severing the land so Dún Briste

comes into play, the old chieftain stranded
among squawking seagulls, left to starve as he leans
on his crooked stick, the waves lashing
far below – a toggle of banished snakes – against

the sea-stack. Or, because speech is buffeted
by the wind, or the telling of ages bound
to distort, or because you are subject to the ground
where you stand, you hear the legend

differently. No pagan, but an ogre, Geodruisge,
pesters the saint, whose prayers are met
when the ogre is cut off from the mainland. One way,
another, twisty and vertiginous as Mayo's

north cliff coast, the spell is cast, and we fall
for everything it has to say, even for the monstrous
overnight storm of 1393 – which split
the stones, stamped its own truth on the chronicle.

Petrosmatoglyphs

This footprint marks the landing of an incredible hulk
of a saint who bounded, centuries ago, clear
across the bay. Or there is the devil's hoof stamped
on granite, the sandal of a warrior king's horse,
the hollow left by a hermit's hand, the divot of kneecap
or elbow plunging him into the gear of his prayer.
Life, we agree, must have felt larger then, the wilderness
greening a path to every door, the cave or mountain
conceived as the first child, the oldest mother.
But tonight, with hay and tar smells tickling the air,
and moon making for the only clock, we find ourselves
yielding to traceries – lip, ear, breast, buttock –
left by two long-lost, runaway lovers on a bed of rock.

Travel

'Choo choo,' he says, watching a steam locomotive
scuttle through the bulging smoke
that fills his TV screen; 'choo choo, choo choo,'
the same sound over and over –
who dreams of driving a bus to town, a taxi
round the houses, who waves
from the windy pier on a day trip to Dún Laoghaire
at the ferry that hoots as it reverses
out the arms of the harbour. Or again his hand
will lift, become a plane's slow
and burdened take-off; but what sends him farthest
is the 'black sun' of starlings
confounding the red-patched sky above the hospital
on autumn evenings: he sits
motionless in his wheelchair gazing up
at the synchronised swirl their flight patterns make –
funnels, wedges, parabolas
locked into the shape and shapelessness
of a time machine, the swift and slow of it, the busy
going somewhere that is his
and for keeps, dancing behind his self-surprising eyes.

Another Life

He's here, the chilly air fringing his grouchiness.
'Thirty years,' he says, 'hauling coal.'
Enough to wear the heart, and the fireplace, out.

You clear a path for him in his stooped blunder
through the house, the wind funnelling
and every photo and figurine threatening take-off.

Bag after bag he empties with a flurried
thrum into the sooty bin – compacted 'nuggets',
'gems' the shape and size of goose eggs.

You pick one up. It feels silken to your fingertips,
yet induces an itch. Its metallic gleam
suggests a meteoroid fire-balling through space.

But you dream the ancient subterraneum
of which it formed part, forests flooded and sunken,
made to simmer in vast, shallow lakes.

Peat, lignite, coal coming about. No help found
in the slow burn of regret if now, again,
forests must drown, the land be over-swept.

'Thirty years,' he reiterates. 'I started early, kept
going.' You attempt camaraderie, recall
summers you spent doing man-labour too young,

in lost bogs of Killoran and Gleann. The sleán
was an education; the books would carry more weight.
He stands, thin as a waif. His hand trembles

as he drains a glass of orange juice. The whites
of his eyes set against his coal-dust face
look immaculate, say, as a Sunday shirt, another life.

In the Burncourt Cave

The 'old man's face' on the cave wall
is a happenstance of iron oxide, manganese
and limestone, not a face at all.
Yet children hand-cup their hellos to 'him',
wave in the dark while the older
and more hard-boiled among us look again,

imagining kindness in those features
as worth our striving for. Calcite curtains
draped alien but exquisite in lamp-lit
grottos or alcoves – are they alive that sparkle
and grow? Or stalactites hanging
from a ceiling – each matchstick-thin, each

set to extend an inch every millennium
until grown at last to resemble
the twisty 'Tower of Babel' or the 'Pillars
of Hercules' – does their dying
amount only to a chemical reaction triggered
by the touch of a careless hand?

I listen for old wall-face's say-so or say-no,
but not as I listened in childhood
for the echo of the ring-fort hollow under
my stamping heel, the slurping
of the weed-haired witch I imagined
drinking the sky from the bottom of a well.

I listen and the earth keeps me guessing –
a stranger still, feeling less at home
than the dead tree in the ash pit, the tombstone

at the centre of the wood, the slouchy hills
perpetuating past sunset a faint
ethereal glimmer that yet seems all their own.

Burials

For a while he fascinated us more than any rock star,
the man who chose to be buried alive
in a coffin, a tube of air fed down
to where he lay in the compacted dark, eating his grub,
drinking, doing – we supposed – his business.

Each day we ear-cupped his drone
out of our radio: he told us how it felt – this enterprise
of his, this place he had to go
so dark only a dead man could grow used to it.
He laughed, but his laugh – and his brand of guff –

soon turned wearisome, and frights
he rustled up stopped scaring us, so we switched him off.
Burials we had already seen, our neighbours
huddled while the priest in wind-licked vestments
cast his ashes-to-ashes prayer, the box

lowered, thump and scrape of earth shovelled over it.
Dying people we had visited – hands
clutching at chenille coverlets, wrists contused
with rainbow colours, voices of those who would die
at home falling to mutters. Their eyes

searched us as if we'd come to rob them;
their flab-skinned gullets choked on spittle or their own
sickish air. And when the curtains were drawn
and the clock stopped, we filed in
through the front door, out the back, maybe noting how

the twig of a fir or Sitka spruce stood
magnified against the moon, or how the rain
slanted in 'heavenly approval' of the life the deceased
had led, or hearing the 'is, isn't, is, isn't'
of a bee nuzzling among wallflowers – and we

would marvel at the lightening of our hearts before
a sense of nature's indifference even as it rose
from frost or decay, from hidden predation
shaking the bushes, from the ruin and countermand
of its creation, brought our mortality

again to thought. Stolid, cottage-cramped,
the adults wrapped death in wreaths and rosary beads,
in ritual and alcohol. Maudlin then,
they would beckon us to touch the cold hands
joined, the head barely denting its bolster. Less ghost

than waxwork tingled our fingers; the bed
of conception and of birthing took what it had given.
We would shake our heads at how mostly
people's dying isn't up to them, all fuses blown at once
or lingeringly their lights put out, their last words

a gasped 'What's happening?', as though aware
of the onset of separation, a journey to be travelled far
from faults and foolishness, from
the thing of the body, the world and its functioning.
Yet they would return, speak to us

without so much as bending our ear; they'd perpetuate
a resonance we might fine-tune, carry
consoled, less lonely for the conversation. But they
would never speak as the buried-alive man
had spoken, through a tube or a yoked-up microphone –

even if, as he did, they must fade into the white noise
of distance, of our growing older, threadbare,
apart. We'd sigh and whisper how – more than ever – they
mattered to us now, would joy to be given
one moment enough to clear our throats, satisfy the hurt.

You Call It Charm

Time has cracked a fault line behind the fire,
sprung a belly in the ceiling, pushed
off-course the once-flush walls. It's entered
in the shape of ivy through a window

you didn't open, recycling breezes
round stairwells, spreading maps of dampness
on pinewood floors. Its touch
is gentle, for all the harm. You call it charm,

part of the happy history of the house,
atmosphere. You even attribute to it your own
indolence, your gathering vision
of mellow afternoons, ripeness and reward.

Yet you resist, twist against the wherewithal
it possesses to steal your lips,
confound your very breath, coming
as a long-cherished lover with dusty fingertips.

However the Malady

However the malady gets in – a shock to the heart,
a wet week or a chink in the skin – however
our lives conspire to kill us, the body falling apart,
the mind worn away, the face of the lover
recognised only on a good day, we pledge even then
to tender these ministrations we make room
for here. Promises we decide never will be broken
yet are not ours for the keeping. A fumblesome
decline draws near. See us suddenly winded,
unmended, sad at how 'our time together just flew'.
But still there is this play of light, the end of it
a ramble along streets to a dwindling path where two
trout leap in the Dodder as it dandles the glow
of the bit moon – tipping its hat, say, to me and you.

'Still it Moves'

It moves, Galileo – the world, the universe, the billions
on billions of miles of observational space
still expanding, Edward Hubble says, and still we imagine
we are the life and soul, the one sentient hub
of the place. Still we look up, look anew – of a day
to read the weather, of a night to lose ourselves
in the hush that comes over us, call it wonderment
waiting to be met. A giant tortoise serving as a griddle
for the flat plate of the earth – not even as children
did we fancy there was that. But Ptolemy
we could picture – in our gripping of stars and planets
each to its approved spot on classroom walls
with blue-tack, or in the hoodwink of the heavens
as undeviating, before we learned how Copernicus had run
those circles in orderly courses about the sun.
You, then, never allowed out again because you dared
to let unwanted truths in; still Jupiter juggles
its moons just as you saw them, still the dance continues
after you've gone; after Newton's apple
hasn't clocked him on the head but 'occasion'd'
his notions about gravity; after Einstein has theorised
on what 'speed' can mean and 'spacetime' do;
after Hawking and co envisage tying together the job lot,
huge with minuscule, while stirring string theory
into the cosmological pot. Meanwhile, for me, this night
waits to be taken to bed. Maybe I'll dream
the twelve-ton 'Leviathan of Parsonstown' I saw today,
whose cooped pine boards – painted black –
set me thinking of a barrel to beat all barrels, our island's
once-upon-a-time world's biggest telescope,
the way it bulges at the middle as though it's gulped a deep
draught of space; dream the heavens as they shift

through its original speculum-metal eye
and how the faraway look we feel we inherit or are given to
holds us fervent, tranquil while the weight
of the world and its troubles in our watching seems to lift.

Vixen

She is the one washed across the River Dodder,
fur plastered to her skin and on her face
a rictus grin, the one yet making her rounds
unfazed by thump or roar of motorcycle
or by ambulance's blue flickering hullaballoo, its
red tinging, and she perpetuates the one
leaping through a net-wire henhouse window
fifty years ago, the cub my neighbour fed
from a trough after he had killed her mother,
the cuddlesome one soon to tune in
to her own feral nature; she absconds, vagabond
at home among the urban – the long
rout of foxes gone before seems to become her,
those dug out, those poisoned or shot
or mangled by hounds, those broken
under the wheels of cars; survivor, the glisten
of health attends her, the youthful lustre
she won't outwear, being too wild, too crossed
with the cricks and crimps of her kin;
she's a fire, an aura, a lollop along the back lane
from dustbin to doorstep, a den dweller,
my first Galway Blazer, my townland-namer,
and it's as if the stars have fashioned
a pelt for her, the frosts a carry, the hills a cover;
as darkness deepens, she comes brushed
with heather smell, harebell, stone-quarry dust,
comes maybe to shake loose her shrieky
mating ochoons or the chalk of cemetery bones –
this numinous one representing all, this
watcher whom I suddenly want to get next to
as though she were the burning down of my years
so lightly here and gone as I take the air
in midsummer, in a midnight suburb of Dublin.

NOTES

p. 23   'Poultice': The Greenland white-fronted goose is sometimes described in our local Callows and bogs as the 'Goose of Ireland'. The word 'whaup', chiefly used in Scotland, refers to the Eurasian curlew.

p. 31   *Fulacht fiadh:* mid to late Bronze Age archaeological sites in Ireland are believed to have been used primarily for cooking meat.

p. 45   ' *Sumer is Icumen in'* is a traditional medieval English round of the mid-13th century and is possibly the oldest known surviving example of independent melodic counterpoint.

p. 49   *Oisín,* meaning 'little deer', is derived from the Irish *os* combined with a diminutive suffix. In Irish legend Oisín was a Gaelic warrior hero and a poet. He is said to have grown suddenly old on his return from Tír na nÓg, the Land of Youth, when his foot accidentally touched the ground as he leaned from his horse to help some men who were trying to lift a heavy stone.

p. 65   Crocodilopolis – one of Egypt's oldest cities – was so named by the Greeks because of its cult of crocodile worship. Its present-day name is Al-Fayoum.

p. 67   Old Croghan Man is the name given to a well-preserved Iron Age body found in Croghan Hill, County Offaly in 2003.

p. 71   The Battle of Aughrim, 12th July 1691, one of the bloodiest in Irish history, was the decisive battle of the Williamite War in Ireland. The Jacobite forces of James 11, led by the Marquis de St Ruth, were defeated by the armies of William 111, commanded by General Godert de Ginkell.

p. 81   *Dún Briste:* 'The Broken Fort', a sea stack situated at Downpatrick Head, Ballycastle, County Mayo.

p. 97   'Still it Moves' is a phrase supposed by some to have been uttered by Galileo in 1633 when he was forced by the Roman Church to recant his claims that the Earth moves around the Sun rather than the converse.

ACKNOWLEDGEMENTS

Acknowledgements are due to the editors and producers of the following where a number of these poems, or versions of them, originally appeared:

Arc Poetry Magazine (Canada); *The Rialto; Envoi; The French Literary Review; Cyphers; The Irish Times; Orbis; The SHOp; Poetry Ireland Review; Southword; Numéro Cinq; The Irish Literary Times; Causeway/Cabhsair* (Aberdeen); *The Ogham Stone; The Tangerine; The Irish Literary Review; Artis Natura* (Ontario); *Skylight 47; The Galway Review; A New Ulster; The Curlew; SurVision Magazine; Eunoia Review* (Singapore); *Tales from the Forest; The Moth Magazine; Into the Void; Algebra of Owls; Southbank Poetry (London); Crannóg; The North* (Sheffield); *The American Journal of Poetry; The Stinging Fly; The Fiddlehead* (New Brunswick); *Ink, Sweat and Tears; The Cannon's Mouth* (Birmingham); *The Stony Thursday Book; Scintilla: The Journal of the Vaughan Association; Prole* (Wales); *Qutub Minar Review* (India); *Silver Streams Journal; Step Away Magazine* (Newcastle upon Tyne); *Poetry Salzburg Review; Rochford Street Review* (Australia).

Some of the poems were included in the following anthologies: *Driftfish: A Zoomorphic Anthology,* edited by Susan Richardson and James Roberts; *The Backyards of Heaven: an anthology of poetry from Ireland and Newfoundland & Labrador,* edited by John Ennis and Stephanie McKenzie (WIT); *WOW! Anthology 2015* (Words on the Waves); *And Other Poems,* an online anthology, edited by Josephine Corcoran; *Between the Leaves,* edited by Anatoly Kudryavitsky (Arlen House); *Teachers Who Write – An Anthology,* edited by Edward Denniston (WTC); *The Lighter Craft: A Festschrift for Peter Denman,* edited by Chris Morash (Astrolabe Press); *Poets for Politics Anthology 2018* (Hungry Hill Writing); *Reading the Future: New Writing from Ireland,* edited by Alan Hayes (Arlen House). 'Vixen' won the inaugural Dermot Healy Poetry Prize in 2014. 'Amcotts Moor Woman' won the 2015 WOW! 2 Award. Other poems which won prizes or were short-listed include 'Shiners', 'Esther' and 'Till the Next Time'.

My sincere gratitude to Judy Carroll Deeley, Genevieve Deeley, Alan Deeley and Michael Nolan for all their encouragement and advice. Special thanks to Pat Boran, editor at Dedalus Press, for his care and attention in publishing this book. I am very grateful to the Arts Council of Ireland/An Chomhairle Ealaíon, for the award of a Bursary in Literature 2017.